Illustrated TAROT SPREADS

Heidemarie Pielmeier
Markus Schirner

Sterling Publishing Co., Inc.
New York

Library of Congress Cataloging-in-Publication Data Available

10 9 8 7 6 5

Published by Sterling Publishing Co., Inc.

387 Park Avenue South, New York, N.Y. 10016

Originally published under the title *Tarot—Welten*, Darmstadt, Germany, © 1995 by Schirner Verlag

English translation © 1999 by Sterling Publishing Co., Inc.

Distributed in Canada by Sterling Publishing

c/o Canadian Manda Group, One Atlantic Avenue, Suite 105

Toronto, Ontario, Canada M6K 3E7

Distributed in Great Britain by Chrysalis Books Group PLC

The Chrysalis Building, Bramley Road, London W10 6SP, England

Distributed in Australia by Capricorn Link (Australia) Pty Ltd.

P.O. Box 704, Windsor, NSW 2756, Australia

Printed in China

Sterling ISBN 0-8069-6345-X

Contents

Partnership

Aids for Decision Making, Problem Solving, and the Oracle

Environment, Occupation, and Success

Introduction

The Tarot and its symbols have existed from time immemorial in the minds and souls of human beings, but not until papermaking and printing became established in Europe was it possible to portray those mighty symbols on cards. Their meanings were known to medieval people, most of whom were illiterate, through the processions that took place in the courtyards of castles. Thus, the first Tarot cards had neither numbers nor letters.

The processions moved around the courtyard in a circular motion, which suggests the symbolism of the wheel. So it is not surprising that "The Wheel of Fortune" card (or "La Fortune") corresponds to the number 10 — which is the 1 plus the 0, indicating that the circle has been completed one time.

The circle moved from left to right, counterclockwise, an allusion to the ages of the world, with its divisions lasting about 2100 years. After the Age of Pisces, for example, we enter the Age of Aquarius. Because of that backwards motion, many people believed that the Tarot should be read backwards, from the last card to the first. But the Tarot forms a circle, and that is why we can enter from any position and jump from one form of development to a totally different one. In the realm of the spirit there can be no hierarchical sequence of the type that human beings invent in order to hold to their logic and reason in the realm of "reality." The Tarot allows us to look beyond logic and to experience a breath of the spirit from which it came.

About A.D.1300, the Tarot was mentioned in an official document, and at the end of that century, the French king Charles VI commissioned cards to be made for a court game. Only a few cards remain from this first set. The deck of cards with the most surviving cards was commissioned around 1450, for the marriage of Bianca Visconti and Francesco Sforza. The background of the colorful, hand-painted cards is of chiseled gold leaf. Because of the expense of producing the cards, they were probably never used. A reprint of this deck is available today. The missing cards were artfully replaced by Luigi Scapini. It is the Visconti-Sforza deck.

In western Europe, during the late Middle Ages and up until the Age of Enlightenment, many card games were printed based on the model of the first French deck. Spelling mistakes came about because the first typesetters were sometimes illiterate.

In 1781, Count de Gebelin discovered connections between the allegories of the game and the Egyptian teachings of initiation, the Book of Thoth. Even though these connections have not been proven, there is little doubt that there is a link to the collective unconscious.

Since that time, occultists have been drawn to the Tarot — including such famous names as Eliphas Levi, Etteilla, Papus, Oswald Wirth, the Order of the Golden Dawn, Aleister Crowley, and Arthur E. Waite. In many countries the fascination with the Tarot never lessened. In others, it resurfaced in the 1960s, among those who tried to better understand the meaning of life and the expansion of consciousness.

Today the Rider-Waite deck is the most popular and widely known pack. It has the advantage of having pictures on all the cards, which makes for easier interpretation. Recently, many other decks have been published, all trying to embellish the cards in different ways, but still in accord with their meanings. We leave it up to you to find the Tarot cards that attract you most.

Often, using two or even more decks will help you to strengthen your associations. Some people work with several decks in order to inspire their soul with more pictures. Our souls love images, but today we have, to a large degree, blocked access to the soul and the handling of symbols. Strengthened by the picture material, we can slowly reopen the choked access. Through this process, the Tarot images will find corresponding reflections in our souls and free us to use our abilities again.

We hope that you, while reading and laying out the cards, will communicate with the pictures in your soul with the help of the Tarot, and that you will enjoy its effect on your life.

Heidemarie Pielmeier
Markus Schirner

How to Use the Tarot

Laying out the Tarot cards is not a quick game. There is no "instant oracle" that presents miracle solutions to all problems. But Tarot cards can certainly be a valuable tool, useful in making decisions, helping you search for the meaning of life, and leading to self-discovery.

The cards show us mirror reflections of ourselves in the outside world. That is why interpretations by others — in books, for example — can be no more than points of reference or notes for setting in motion our own chain of associations. The meanings of the individual cards are to be found in ourselves. We need to investigate the cards with the help of the responses they evoke in us. It is important to remember that the cards only reveal possibilities, which don't necessarily have to materialize, because we ourselves are the masters of our fate, and shape and direct it.

After you have decided on a certain kind of Tarot deck and have taken it home, don't lay it out immediately. First, get to know it. Go through the deck off and on, and look at the cards, until you gradually get to know their names and numbers and develop a feel for them.

It's a good idea to start a "card diary," in which you jot down the thoughts that come to mind when you look at the individual cards. In this way, you will create your very own book of interpretations. It will serve you well.

When you put the cards aside, choose a special cloth to wrap them in. Select a cloth you would later want to use for laying out the cards. Always spread the cards yourself, because over time the cards will become a part of you. No one else should handle them.

When you finally start to lay out your cards, begin with small spreads. Increase the number of cards gradually: this way they will grow on you, so to speak, "organically."

For the time being, put aside all books of interpretations and listen to your inner self, noting down your impressions in your card diary. Later, consult a book of interpretations and find further inspirations.

Before you get started, provide for an undisturbed setting. Turn off the buzzer and the phone, close the door, and if necessary lock it. Tell the people living with you that you would like to be left alone for a while. After quiet has been established on the outside, you need to become quiet on the inside. To achieve this, simple measures are often the best, like practicing deep abdominal breathing for a few counts, imagining that you are sitting next to a lake in the golden light of dusk, or drinking a cup of tea — use whatever you know will put you into a peaceful mood.

Next, fill your mind with the question for which you want to consult the cards. Let as many images as possible come to your mind about this question. Then, distance yourself again from your theme, and try to take as neutral a position as possible.

Pick up the stack of cards and shuffle it. By the way, the most effective way to handle the cards is to mix them on the cloth by pushing them upwards, face down, and then shuffling them with both hands. Mix the cards until you have the feeling it is enough. Afterwards, push the cards together into a neat stack, and set it on the cloth in front of you. With your left hand, lift off a part of the stack and place it to the left of the first stack. If you are using the Major Arcana only, simply take the first stack and place it on the second, and you will be ready to begin. But if you want to use all 78 cards, take off about half of the second stack and put it back on top of the first stack; then take this whole stack and place it on the second stack. Now the cards are shuffled. Spread out the cards like a fan in front of you on the cloth. Without touching the cards, let your left hand glide over them. Before you make a selection, wait until you "respond" to a card. This can manifest itself by a tingling in the tips of your fingers or a feeling of warmth in your palm. Then place the card on its place in the layout. Repeat the procedure as often as you need cards.

When you start turning over the cards — one at a time — it's best to turn them from left to right. That is especially important if you would like to work on the interpretation of each "reversed" card, which, by the way, is not at all mandatory. Don't turn over all the cards at once, but only one after the other.

Before you arrive at an interpretation, listen to your inner self about what the cards have to tell you. Here the numerous symbols pictured on the cards will help you. Often the essential clue is in a detail; a color or an object might put you on the right track. Then, use the suggestions you will find in Tarot instruction books as an anchor to go into even deeper waters. And always be sure to question your own answers.

If all the cards are facing up, try to connect the individual interpretations you found and thus, carefully approach a solution. Note it down in your card diary. Gather experience; it will be continually helpful to you.

After you are finished, shuffle all the cards once more, and wrap them, stacked neatly, in the cloth and put them back in their place. If you have the feeling once in a while that you would like to put them in order again, then stack them in the correct order, Major Arcana (0–21) and Minor Arcana (Wands, Cups, Swords, and Coins or Pentacles), starting with the lowest number. Leave them this way for a while. It will restore order once more.

The Tarot cards are like Ariadne's magic thread, leading us — by the way we are able to touch and hold them — from the labyrinth of confusion to the daylight of clarity.

How to Use This Book

From a simple three-card spread to a complex layout with 34 cards, this book offers the beginner as well as the advanced student ways to achieve a better understanding of yourself, your partner, your environment, and your life situation.

It presupposes a beginning knowledge of the Tarot cards and their meanings, but it contains short interpretations that allow for a quick check.

You will see a Sum of the Digits card mentioned. It is found by adding up the total numbers of the cards in a spread. For the Major Arcana, use the numbers that appear on the card. For the Minor Arcana, there are two groups: the numbered cards and the cards of the court — Page, Knight, Queen, and King. All cards of the court count 0. So, in a three-card spread, you might have a Two of Wands (2), a Page of Pentacles (0), and The Star (17). You would add 2 to 0 to 17, and that would add up to 19. You would then reduce the 19 (1 + 9) to 10, and reduce again (1 + 0), to 1. This card will give you guidance on how to act in a certain situation.

* * * * *

From a separate table (see page 15), you can choose the card that corresponds to your birthday. In a reading, these are key cards, and they have a personal meaning for you.

More than fun and games in the process of self discovery, this book also shows how to recognize the seriousness of a situation and helps you to act with appropriate responsibility.

A Short Interpretation of the Tarot Cards

THE MAJOR ARCANA

1 The Magician
   The Conjuror
    will
   strong ego
   consciousness
   magic work
   gradual change
   illusions
   betrayal
   talks

2 The High Priestess
    knowledge beyond intuition
   hidden wisdom
   intuition
   instructive dreams
   spirituality
   divine laws
   divination
   bigotry
   silence

3 The Empress
    generosity
   motherhood
   creativity
   refinement
   zest for life
   inertia
   prudery
   gossip

4 The Emperor
    father figure
   positive force (power)
   benefactor
   diplomas
   obstacles
   stubbornness

5 The Hierophant
   The High Priest
    religion
   education
   marriage
   service
   obligations
   hypocrisy

6 The Lovers
    partnership
   love
   contradictions
   decisions

7 The Chariot
    compromise
   certainty of victory
   vitality
   former mistakes

8 Strength
    discipline
   strength of mind
   success through willpower
   firm actions
   passion

9 The Hermit
    kindness
   inner strength
   wisdom
   silence
   caution
   slow effectiveness

10 The Wheel
    of Fortune
    luck
    turning to goodness
    optimism
    sudden change

11 Justice
    balanced justice
    end of conflict
    harmony
    bigotry

12 The Hanged Man
    intuitive wisdom
    inner processes
    personal sacrifice

enlightenment
déjà vu experience
to let oneself go

13	Death The Card Without a Name	renewal loss critical change change of current life circumstances new growth following departure (leave-taking)
14	Temperance	purity clarification highest psychic ability adaptation solitude (desert)
15	The Devil	temptation power obsession uncovered vice dependence imprisonment monotonous studies emotional ties to an indifferent person obsession with work humor
16	The Tower	sudden catastrophes revolution opposition cleansing actions thrust of evolution
17	The Star	spiritual vision questions about meanings birth independence influence on others
18	The Moon	intuition gradual change change in personality

hidden enemies
hard-to-understand
(incomprehensible) forces

19	The Sun	unification contentment success in business journeys higher (heightened) consciousness freedom
20	Judgment Resurrection	rebirth important decisions important change memories forgotten dreams and goals can taken up again — old parts of the personality come to the surface
21	The World The Universe	realization developed freedom to become famous due to creativity communication journeys
0	The Fool	new cycle ideals risk swiftness vanity foolishness

MINOR ARCANA

Court Cards

Page of Wands	stranger glad tidings small journeys the essence of personality new job superficiality

Knight of Wands	change
	departure
	change of residence
	change of occupation
	the body of the personality
	dangerous atmosphere
Queen of Wands	passion
	magic
	mediumistic abilities
	the soul of the personality
	success in business
	domineering
King of Wands	readiness for departure
	faithfulness
	overexertion
	the ego of the personality
	chance
	unexpected inheritance
	daredevil
Page of Cups	love letters
	devotion
	enjoyment
	meditation
	talents
	deceptive offers
	desire for luxury
Knight of Cups	romance
	arrival
	new lover
	invitation
	proposal
	flight into the dream world
	deception
Queen of Cups	sensuousness
	tenderness
	mediumistic qualities
	luck

	joy
	seduction
	malice
	dishonesty
King of Cups	mildness
	generosity
	artist
	good advice
	kindness
	hidden violence
	danger of drug addiction
	easily seduced
Page of Swords	investigations
	supervisor
	observer
	agility
	indiscretion
	conflict
Knight of Swords	fighter
	helpful in controversies
	aggressiveness
	revenge
	destruction
	fall in temperature
Queen of Swords	intelligence
	sadness
	loneliness
	cynicism
King of Swords	sternness
	authority
	institutions
	egoism
	lawsuit
	tyranny
	unfaithfulness
Page of Pentacles (Coins)	studies, apprentice
	seriousness

	novelties
	news about money
	employment contract
	waste
	bribery
Knight of Pentacles (Coins)	stability
	gain—luck in money matters
	responsibility
	regulated life style
	stubbornness
	arrested development
Queen of Pentacles (Coins)	loving care
	taking possession
	abundance
	marriage
	moods
	wastefulness
	desire for money
	lack of imagination
King of Pentacles (Coins)	stability
	master
	dexterity
	laziness
	corruption
	jealousy

Numbered Cards

Ace of Wands	spark
	birth, growth
	fruitfulness
	overreaction
Two of Wands	partnership
	big plans
	indecision
Three of Wands	wait and see
	responsibility
	enterprise
Four of Wands	arrival
	luck
	beauty
	joy
	finished work
Five of Wands	resistance
	ambition
	competitive fights
Six of Wands	conquest
	triumph
	successful completion of a project
Seven of Wands	critique
	overcoming
	courage
	negotiations
	success in holding out
Eight of Wands	swiftness
	the garden
	hectic
	many irons in the fire
Nine of Wands	pause
	lateness
	vigilance
	looking for trouble
	no enjoyment of safe circumstances
Ten of Wands	overburden
	search
	pressure due to wrong attitude
Ace of Cups	richness of feeling
	overflowing emotions
	fertility
Two of Cups	love
	mutual interests
	exchange of loving energy

Three of Cups	overabundance success lucky turn fun
Four of Cups	satiety (ennui) boredom unable to be enthusiastic
Five of Cups	remorse inheritance disappointment
Six of Cups	looking back oriented towards the past constant (steady) growth
Seven of Cups	imagination trickery many goals are a waste of time
Eight of Cups	parting virginity search for higher meaning
Nine of Cups	physical well-being victory everything is airtight
Ten of Cups	peace family happiness harmonious partnership
Ace of Swords	freedom of thought vibration overcoming conquest
Two of Swords	doubt alliance armistice to be in the dark

Three of Swords	heartbreak disagreement sorrow
Four of Swords	recovery excommunication plans of revenge manifest them- selves in daydreams
Five of Swords	relapse loss slander
Six of Swords	flight difficult path journey by water
Seven of Swords	cunning hope small victory
Eight of Swords	limitation difficulties being on edge
Nine of Swords	panic feeling of shame illness
Ten of Swords	betrayal sadness end of an illusion failure
Ace of Pentacles (Coins)	fulfillment of wish satisfaction new financial start help in an undertaking
Two of Pentacles (Coins)	game surprise juggling finances income of an artist/performer

Third of Pentacles (Coins)	success completion status
Four of Pentacles (Coins)	settlement good deed property material success
Five of Pentacles (Coins)	poverty lover a new way of living difficult circumstances
Six of Pentacles (Coins)	gift largess luck in games unexpected gift of money
Seven of Pentacles (Coins)	strife growth delays in money matters passing depression
Eight of Pentacles (Coins)	work endurance new techniques money path to the goal
Nine of Pentacles (Coins)	prosperity neglect of the partner for financial reasons completion of work relaxation
Ten of Pentacles (Coins)	house family inheritance perfection material gain tradition being hemmed in

Sum of the Digits Card

This card can be determined at the end of various Tarot readings. It provides advice on how best to treat the situation that is the theme of the reading. It is the essence of the interpretation. See page 7 for instructions on finding the Sum of the Digits Card.

1 The Magician
It is up to you to explore all the possibilities and to influence fate through your will. You are agile and know how to arrange matters so that they will be advantageous for you.

2 The High Priestess
Listen to your intuition. Do not act, but wait. Everything is proceeding according to your wishes.

3 The Empress
You will solve your problem in a feminine manner. Calm and love, gregariousness and joy are your weapons. Show confidence in your creativity.

4 The Emperor
Now you can introduce structure and order into your life. Be active and ambitious. Dreaming will not help you. Start acting.

5 The Hierophant
Look beyond the secret of the current situation. You know the meaning of the past, present, and future. Have confidence in the divine advisor who resides within you.

6 The Lovers
Be ready for love. It will open all doors for you and will give back to you. Make a decision joyfully. Every path is the correct one. Be prepared for a union.

7 The Chariot
Approach your goal with composure. You are responsible for your life — nobody else is. With the certainty that you will be victorious, you can achieve everything.

8 Strength

Your strength will help you in anything you want to achieve. Don't force yourself. Let your enjoyment of life conquer all inconveniences and adversity. Turn your power to the outside. Show what you are capable of.

9 The Hermit

Love solitude. In seclusion, you will find the values important to your life. Strive for them.

10 The Wheel of Fortune

Learn how to flow with the ups and downs of life. Don't complain, but change your attitude. Resistance will produce disturbance.

11 Justice

Your judgment has to be objective, but do not judge. Believe in the higher justice that rules you. Remember: What you give will come back to you.

12 The Hanged Man

Turn around. Look at yourself through the eyes of others. Change your attitude. Give without expecting anything in return. Be ready for sacrifice.

13 Death

Renounce your fear of the unchangeable; it is only a passage to a new form of life. Now you will get your second chance. Let go of the old in order to grasp this chance.

14 Temperance

Don't be extreme. Choose the middle path. Cool off. Get on top of the situation. Observe and let your intuition work. Prepare a new mixture. The alchemist in you knows that the mixture has to simmer for a long time to bring forth something precious.

15 The Devil

Be honest with yourself. Get to know your shadow side, your dependence, and your addictions. Observe your desire for power. You too have it. If you can admit to it, you can free yourself and be kinder to fellow human beings.

16 The Tower

Now it is time to clean out and open up for new ways. You possess an enormous amount of energy and can shake up yourself and your environment. Do it yourself; otherwise, somebody else will do it for you, and that will not be pleasant. You can leave your prison, relieved of a lot of burdens.

17 The Star

Never lose hope. You will always get what you need. In infinity there is consolation for you, too. Compose yourself and be full of confidence.

18 The Moon

If you are dreaming, and know that you are dreaming, you can perceive the deception in your environment. The dark forces of the night can't touch you, if you look them straight in the eye. Here, in your own depths, you are able to see your true self.

19 The Sun

You are successful and will grow in your occupation. With courage and confidence, you can achieve anything in life. The Sun is lighting every path. Keep to your resolution.

20 Judgment

Now you will get your reward. Everything that caused you trouble before will disappear. You don't have to worry about everyday life any longer. Things you need will be given to you by higher powers.

21 The World

You are in harmony with yourself and the universe. You united the polarities in yourself. The whole world is at your feet. Through your own power, you achieved more than you'd hoped for. Enjoy your achievements. Adapt to the force of life. Travel around the world.

0 The Fool

Be open to the gift of life. Experience the moment spontaneously. Look to the future and follow the way of your heart.

Your Personal Tarot Card
- based on your birth date -

CORRESPONDING TO THE MINOR ARCANA

March 21	0° Aries/Easter	Page of Wands	Queen of Wands
March 22 - 30	2 of Pentacles	2 of Wands	Queen of Wands
March 31 - April 10	3 of Pentacles	3 of Wands	Queen of Wands
April 11 - 20	4 of Pentacles	4 of Wands	Queen of Wands
April 21 - 30	5 of Pentacles	5 of Pentacles	King of Pentacles
May 1	10° Taurus/Beltane	Ace of Pentacles	King of Pentacles
May 2 - 10	6 of Pentacles	6 of Pentacles	King of Pentacles
May 11 - 20	7 of Pentacles	7 of Pentacles	King of Pentacles
May 21 - 31	8 of Pentacles	8 of Swords	Knight of Swords
June 1 - 10	9 of Pentacles	9 of Swords	Knight of Swords
June 11 - 20	10 of Pentacles	10 of Swords	Knight of Swords
June 21	0° Cancer/St. John's Day	Page of Cups	Queen of Cups
June 22 - July 1	2 of Wands	2 of Cups	Queen of Cups
July 2 - 11	3 of Wands	3 of Cups	Queen of Cups
July 12 - 21	4 of Wands	4 of Cups	Queen of Cups
July 22 - 31	5 of Wands	5 of Wands	King of Wands
August 1	10° Leo/Lughnasa	Ace of Wands	King of Wands
August 2 - 11	6 of Wands	6 of Wands	King of Wands
August 12 - 22	7 of Wands	7 of Wands	King of Wands
August 23 - September 1	8 of Wands	8 of Pentacles	Knight of Pentacles
September 2 - 11	9 of Wands	9 of Pentacles	Knight of Pentacles
September 12 - 22	10 of Wands	10 of Pentacles	Knight of Pentacles
September 23	0° Libra/Autumnal equinox	Page of Swords	Queen of Swords
September 24 - October 2	2 of Cups	2 of Swords	Queen of Swords
October 3 - 12	3 of Cups	3 of Swords	Queen of Swords
October 13 - 22	4 of Cups	4 of Swords	Queen of Swords
October 23 - 31	5 of Cups	5 of Cups	King of Cups
November 1	10° Scorpio/Samhain	Ace of Cups	King of Cups
November 2 - 12	6 of Cups	6 of Cups	King of Cups
November 13 - 22	7 of Cups	7 of Cups	King of Cups
November 23 - Dec. 2	8 of Cups	8 of Wands	Knight of Wands
December 3 - 12	9 of Cups	9 of Wands	Knight of Wands
December 13 - 21	10 of Cups	10 of Wands	Knight of Wands
December 22	0° Capricorn/Yule festival	Page of Pentacles	Queen of Pentacles
December 23 - 30	2 of Swords	2 of Pentacles	Queen of Pentacles
December 31 - January 9	3 of Swords	3 of Pentacles	Queen of Pentacles
January 10 - 19	4 of Swords	4 of Pentacles	Queen of Pentacles
January 20 - 29	5 of Swords	5 of Swords	King of Swords
January 30 - February 1	6 of Swords	6 of Swords	King of Swords
February 2	10° Aquarius/Candlemas	Ace of Swords	King of Swords
February 3 - 8	6 of Swords	6 of Swords	King of Swords
February 9 - 18	7 of Swords	7 of Swords	King of Swords
February 19 - 29	8 of Swords	8 of Cups	Knight of Cups
March 1 - 10	9 of Swords	9 of Cups	Knight of Cups
March 11 - 20	10 of Swords	10 of Cups	Knight of Cups

CORRESPONDING TO THE MAJOR ARCANA

March 21 - April 20	♈	The Emperor
April 21 - May 20	♉	The Hierophant
May 21 - June 20	♊	The Lovers
June 21 - July 21	♋	The Chariot
July 22 - August 22	♌	Strength
August 23 - September 22	♍	The Hermit
September 23 - October 22	♎	Justice
October 23 - November 22	♏	Death
November 23 - December 21	♐	Temperance
December 22 - January 19	♑	The Devil
January 20 - February 18	♒	The Star
February 19 - March 20	♓	The Moon

Know Thyself

Use this layout no more than once every eight weeks, when you have the feeling that you have taken another step in self-knowledge.

1. Who am I?

2. What do I need?

3. How will I get it?

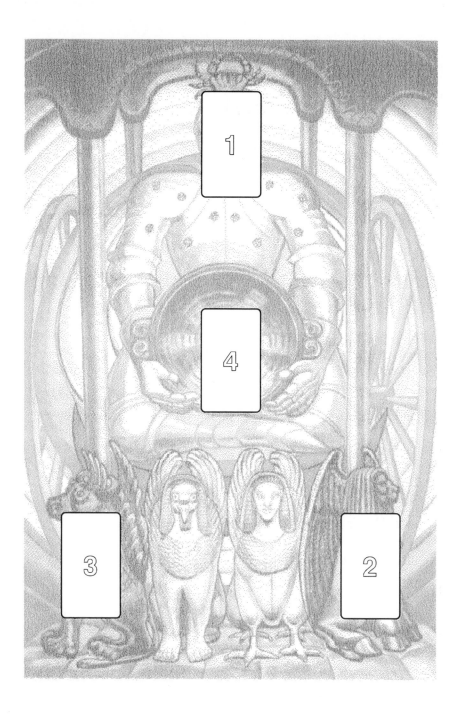

Reaching the Goal

1. My goal

2. What qualities can I use to achieve my goal?

3. What am I doing that prevents me from reaching my goal?

4. How do I reach my goal?

The Celtic Cross

- myself -

1. Myself

2. What my self releases in me

3. What makes me happy

4. What frightens me

5. What slips away from me

6. What I can still hold on to

7. What I am

8. What I am capable of doing

9. What I want

10. What I can finally achieve

11. Where it will lead me

The Druid's Cross

0. The matter under consideration
   This card is drawn either from an open deck or from a covered deck, and it is placed under the first card.

1. What I would like

2. What I do

3. What I reject

4. What I can't get

5. My ideal

6. What I will receive

7. How I present myself

8. How people react to me

9. My hopes and fears

10. How it will end — or continue

Interpretation of Dreams

1. My Dream

   Consciously choose this card from an open Tarot deck. It will be connected with your dream.

2. What past event does the dream relate to?

3. What is the theme of the dream?

4. What is the message of the dream?

5. How shall I respond to the message of the dream?

The Wise Woman

1. My being

2. My actual — or not actual — physical motherhood

3. What did it bring me physically?

4. What did it teach me mentally?

5. This is how I feel now

6. What is my spiritual motherhood (or social or spiritual commitment) going to look like?

7. How will I realize it?

8. What will it bring to me?

9. What will become of me — the wise woman?

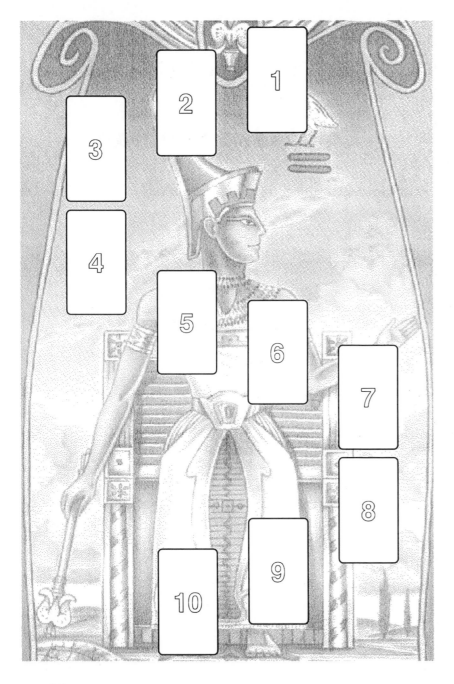

The Tropic of Capricorn

- the turning point of the man -

1. What task did I accomplish?

2. What task awaits me?

3. How strongly am I attracted to this task?

4. What obstacles will I have to face?

5. How much energy will I have to use?

6. Will I do it alone, or with a group?

7. Do I have enough money for the task?

8. Where will the task be resolved?

9. When will it be resolved?

10. What will I gain?

The Tropic of Cancer

- the turning point of the woman -

1. What do I want to change? Or what direction do I want to choose?

2. What obstacles will have to be cleared out of the way?

   What tasks still have to be undertaken?

3. Do I have enough creativity?

4. Will I have the energy I'll need?

5. Do I have the strength or courage to do it alone?

6. Do I have enough money to do it?

7. Am I in the right place?

8. What is the right time?

9. Will I be able to do it?

10. What will I gain personally?

Self-Improvement

- aid to meditation -

1. Who and how am I?

2. How do I want to be?

3. How am I supposed to be?

4. Where did I come from?

5. Where will my destiny lead me?

6. My purpose in life/my mission

7. Help from the spiritual world

8. Help from the soul

Removing the Obstacle

1. The ego (or the problem)

2. The boundaries

3. The fear

4. The denial

5. The inability

6. The desire or lust

7. The feeling of inferiority

8. The vision

9. The initiative

10. The tolerance

11. The willpower

12. The modesty

13. The self-confidence

14. The solution

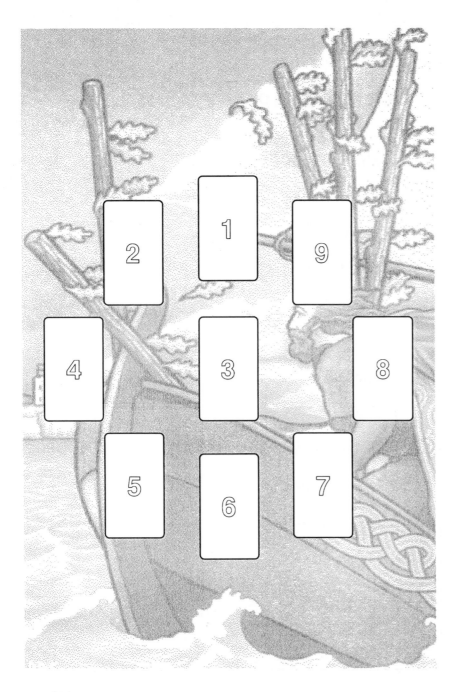

Journey into the Outer Regions

- recognition of the problem -

1. The harbor

    Where I am right now/my current position/where I stand

2. The realm of the rainbow

    The source of my dissatisfaction, my anxiety, or my problem/the reason for my search

3. The realm of the wish

    What I am searching for/my ideal solution/my vision or my dream

4. The realm of terror

    Anxieties and uncertainties; things that are holding me back

5. The realm of youth

    My abilities, possibilities, and talents

6. The realm of the mirror

    Who or what stands in the way

7. The realm of the fairies

    Who or what helps me

8. The realm of miracles

    Valuable gifts from the outer world, or my ancestors helping me/hidden facts becoming visible now

9. Land in sight!
    How will I solve my problem or answer my question?

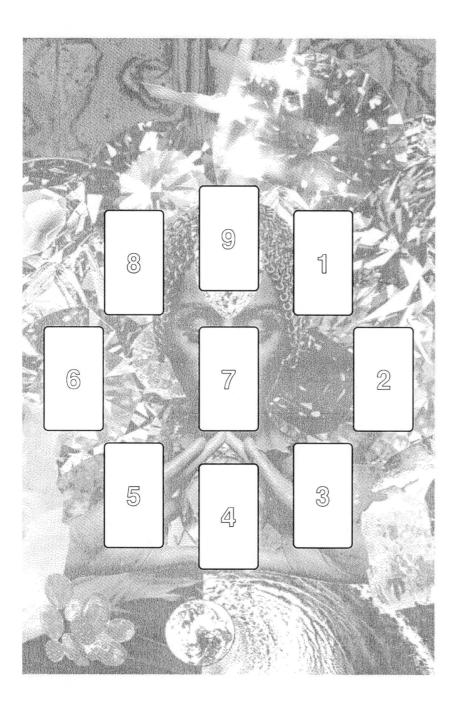

Journey Inside

- how do I continue? -

1. Land in sight! The journey home
   What is the best way for me to act now?

2. The realm of miracles
   Inherited memories/my communication with the divine

   What is the source of the sacred and of wholeness in my life?

3. The realm of the fairies
   Needs and shortcomings

   What is the source of love in my life?

4. The realm of mirrors
   Decisions and difficulties

   What is the source of anxiety in my life?

5. The realm of youth
   Regeneration and renewal

   What is the source of creativity in my life?

6. The realm of terror
   Challenges I will have to overcome

   What is the source of strength in my life?

7. The realm of wishes
   Beauty and harmony

   What is the source of inspiration in my life?

8. The realm of the rainbow
   Change and possibilities

   What is the source of versatility and adaptation in my life?

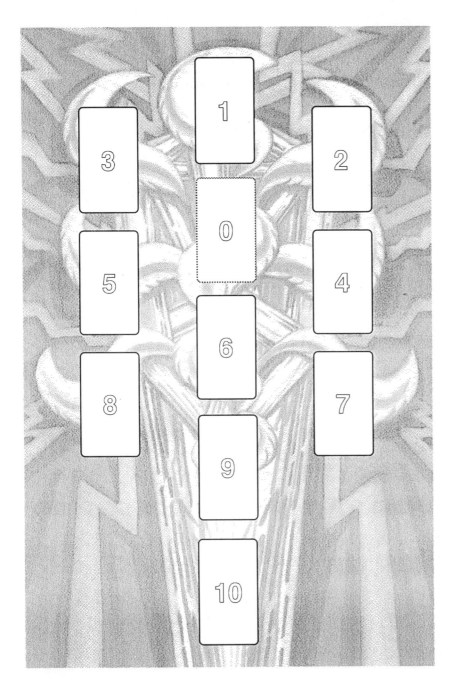

The Tree of Life

- as the Tarot sees it -

1. What do I have to study to make use of the possibilities indicated in position 10?

2. How do I need to handle the obstacles?

3. How dependent am I and how is my ability to let go?

4. My dealings with the necessities of life

   What gifts have I received from the inside and the outside?

5. What do I have to do to clarify grievances?

6. How is my center/my self-contentment?

7. My attitude/my defenses/my prejudices

8. My intention/my deeds

9. This is my unconscious

10. What possibilities are being offered to me in the here and now?

    What do I have to achieve here?

The Tree of Life

- of the seven levels -

1. Level of regeneration
   My ability for regeneration — the possibilities

2. Level of creativity
   My inspiration . . .

3. . . . And its realization

4. Level of occupation
   Limitations and my task

5. Social level
   My kindness — my wild naturalness . . .

6. . . . And its taming — my self-discipline

7. Spiritual level
   My inner self

8. Mental level
   My feeling . . .

9. . . . And my thinking

10. Emotional level
    My psyche — my unconscious

11. Body
    My physical being — a mirror of the environment

Moderation

- *Measure for Measure* -

1. What from my past determines my present?

2. What from my present will I take into the future?

3. Where do I come from? My former actions, my past in the widest sense, including my previous existence

4. Where am I going?
   My destination in the widest sense

5. My spiritual tendencies

   9. How do I actualize them?

6. My worldly tendencies

   10. How do I actualize them?

7. My feelings

   11. How do I actualize them?

8. My environment in the widest sense: the environment I supposedly can't influence — such as television, the media, other countries, and friends, too

12. My environment — in terms of alliances, brother hood, war, market economy, etc.

13. What tendencies or qualities do I need to overcome or discard? Which of these are a hindrance on my path?

14. What qualities do I need to develop to help me on my path — or to construct my path?

Karmic Development

Sort the Tarot cards and make three stacks: Major Arcana/Court Cards/Numbered cards from Ace to 10. Mix these three stacks separately, and then pull:

Cards 1, 4, and 7 from the Major Arcana
Cards 2, 5, and 8 from the Court Cards
Cards 3, 6, and 9 from the numbered cards

Put all the rest of the cards together again, mix, and pull cards 10 and 11.

1. What was my developmental stage in my former life?

2. What role did I play?

3. What was the most important event in my former life?

4. What stage of development describes my current life?

5. What role am I playing right now?

6. Is a former event still influencing me?

7. What inner state of development am I trying to achieve?

8. What other role would also be fitting for me?

9. What event will I encounter in the future?

10. What kind of task will arise from this?

11. How can this knowledge help me in the present?

Health Oracle

1. My physical constitution

2. What strengthens my body?

3. What weakens my body?

4. What am I doing wrong?

5. What am I doing right?

6. Where will my way of life lead?
   What does the oracle say (see 7 and 8)?

7. Point in time

8. Event

Wands	Days
Cups	Weeks
Pentacles	Months
Pages	11
Knights	12
Queens	Wands and Cups 13
Kings	Wands and Cups 14
Queens	Swords and Pentacles: the oracle
+Kings	Silence about the point in time
Swords	The time, starting now
Major Arcana	The hours, starting from now (0 = now; 22 + 23 hours already belong to the Ace of Wands.)

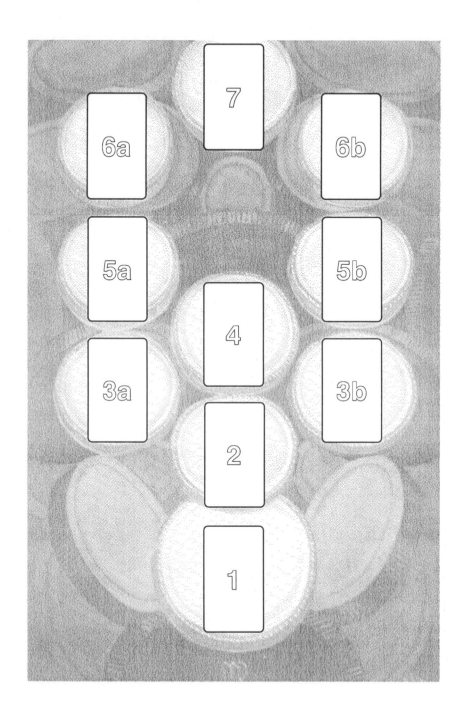

Reading of the Chakras

- state of my health -

1. Root Chakra
   Root of my problem/my habits/my reservoir
   of energy

2. Sexual Chakra
   My sexual energy/my deep-seated emotions and
   feelings

3. Solar Plexus Chakra
   a. My will/my ego   b. My emotional ties

4. Heart Chakra
   My ability to heal myself
   What do I need to accept with unconditional love?

5. Throat Chakra
   a. My inner communication
      What does my inner self have to tell me?
   b. My communication with the outside
      With whom am I truly connected?

6. Third Eye Chakra
   a. My dreams/the right side of my brain
      What do my dreams and intuition tell me?
   b. My possibilities/the left side of my brain
      What desires or wishes have I lost?

7. Crown Chakra
   My highest aims/connection to the beginning
   What will be the result of healing myself?
   What support will I get during the healing process?

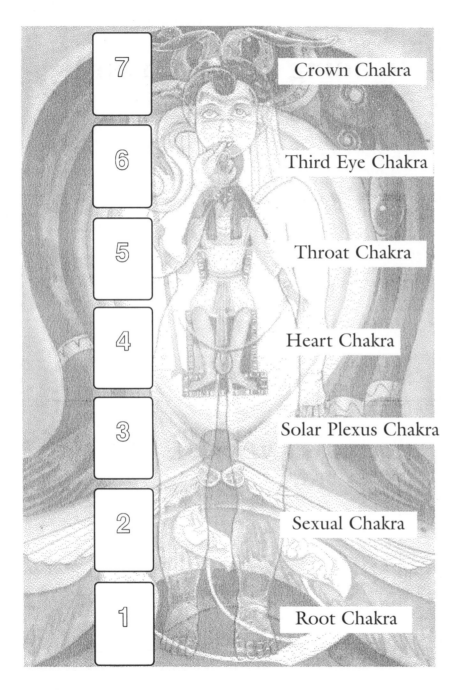

7 — Crown Chakra

6 — Third Eye Chakra

5 — Throat Chakra

4 — Heart Chakra

3 — Solar Plexus Chakra

2 — Sexual Chakra

1 — Root Chakra

Reading of the Chakras

- my body -

1. Root Chakra
   My knowledge of my personality/my willpower/pro-creation/growth/teeth/brain/hair/ears/kidneys/bladder/water balance/respiratory organs/anxiety/stress/insecurity

2. Sexual Chakra
   My resoluteness (goal orientation)/my self-control/organs of elimination/stomach/pancreas/over-acidification/resignation/worries about the future/brooding/suppressed feelings

3. Solar Plexus Chakra
   My ability to be tolerant/my richness of ideas/flow of energy/blood, etc./structure and tendons/nails/adrenal glands/allergies/tiredness/rheumatism/upset/frustrations/existential anxiety

4. Heart Chakra
   My ability to judge/circulatory system/heart/brain/small intestines/nervousness/strong feelings (sadness and joy)

5. Throat Chakra
   My talents in the arts/lungs/nose/throat/thyroid glands/large intestines/skin/disappointment/trouble/sorrow

6. Third Eye Chakra
   My discipline and visions/abstract thought/clairvoyance

7. Crown Chakra
   My desire for understanding/metabolism/energy on a spiritual level

The Gate to Life

- my karma -

1. + 2. What kind of karma am I bringing along from the past?

3. + 4. My highest motivation/my goal

5. + 6. What kind of karma am I generating for the future?

What impediments are still to be overcome . . .

7. . . . in the world of the spirit?

8. . . . in the soul?

9. . . . in the material world?

What help is given to me . . .

10. . . . in the world of the spirit?

11. . . . in the soul?

12. . . in the material world?

13. My qualities/my weakness/my potential

Wish for a Partner

- Will my desire for partnership have a chance in the next six months? -

1. My wish

2. Will I meet my partner?

3. If yes, will I be contented with him?

4. If yes, what positive contributions can I make?

An Alternative

3. If the answer to question 3 is no, is it best for me to stay alone for now?

4. If no, what can I do in order to meet my partner?

5. Sum of the Digits: The advice of the Tarot for my future life concerning partnerships

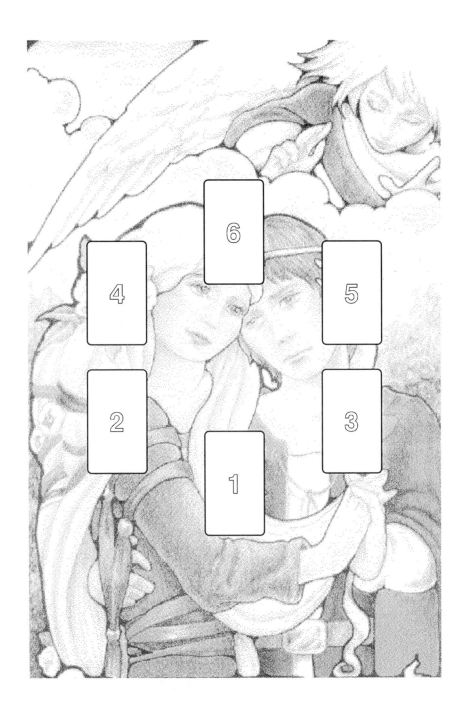

The Soul Mate

1. What does my soul mate look like?

2. How can we meet?

3. What do we have in common?

4. What obstacles still have to be overcome?

5. What kind of task still has to be completed?

6. What does the oracle say about our future together?

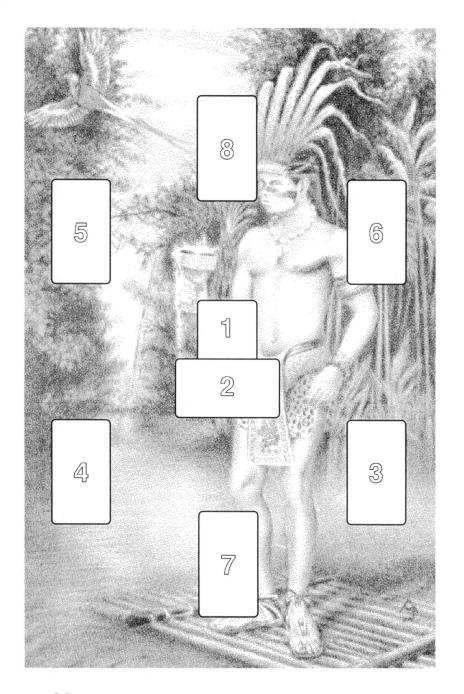

A New Relationship

1. I myself

2. How do I feel consciously about the relationship?

3. How do I feel unconsciously about the relationship?

4. What mistakes from the past should I recognize and clear away?

5. What additional qualities do I need to take on?

6. What positive effect will my change create?

7. What will not happen?

8. What does the oracle say?

A New Partner?

1. What keeps me attached to my old partner?

2. What attracts me to my new partner?

3. What shall I do?

4. How shall I do it?

5. What will I gain?

Partnership

- Recognition -

1. I myself

2. How do I see my partner?

3. How do I see our relationship?

4. This strengthens our relationship

5. This weakens our relationship

6. My hopes

7. My fears

8. My task in the relationship

9. His/her task in the relationship

10. This will come out of it

Analysis of the Partnership

1. The situation
2. Myself in the partnership
3. The other in the partnership
4. Where does the partnership come from?
5. Where is the partnership going?
6. My expectations
7. My fears
8. What do I contribute to the partnership?
9. What do I lack in the partnership? What am I not contributing or giving enough of?
10. The expectations of the partner
11. The fears of the partner
12. What does the other contribute to the partnership?
13. What does the other lack in the partnership? What is he/she not contributing?

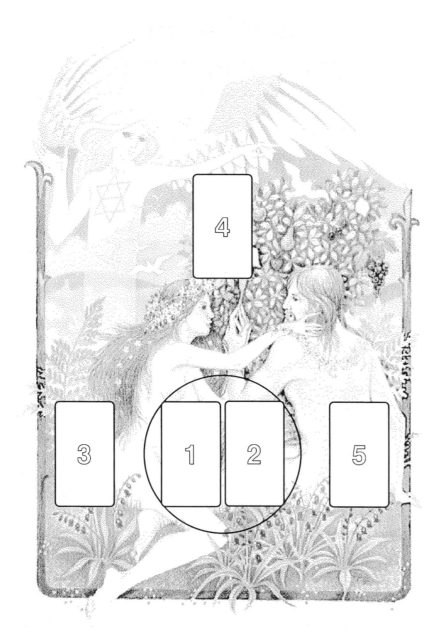

Partnership

- attachment -

1. Myself in the relationship

   How do I see myself?

2. My partner

   How do I see my partner?

3. What bound us together in the past?

4. What keeps us connected in the present?

5. What awaits our future relationship?

Partnership

- love relationship — business relationship -

1. The overall circumstances of the partnership

2. What is my participation in it?

3. What is the participation of the other?

4. This is what I need to bring to the relationship

5. The habits I need to discard

6. Helping Card 1
   This is what will help me in my surroundings

7. Helping Card 2
   This is what will help me in the spiritual world

8. Warning Card 1
   This could cost me the partnership

9. Warning Card 2
   This is obstructive in the partnership

10. How will the partnership continue?

The Enmeshment

- interrelationship -

This reading is done only with the cards of the Major Arcana.

1. How does my partner see me?

2. How do I see myself?

3. How do I see my partner?

4. How does my partner see himself/herself?

5. What do I need to do or not do in our partnership?

6. What will I gain?

7. What is my current level of development?

8. What is the current level of development of my partner?

9. What is our common denominator?
   Sum of the Digits Card!

Partnership

- conflict resolution -

1. The circumstances of our relationship

2. What do I contribute to the relationship?

3. What does my partner contribute to the relationship?

4. What do I need to do — or what can I do — for the relationship?

5. What will my partner do for the relationship?

6. How will our relationship continue?

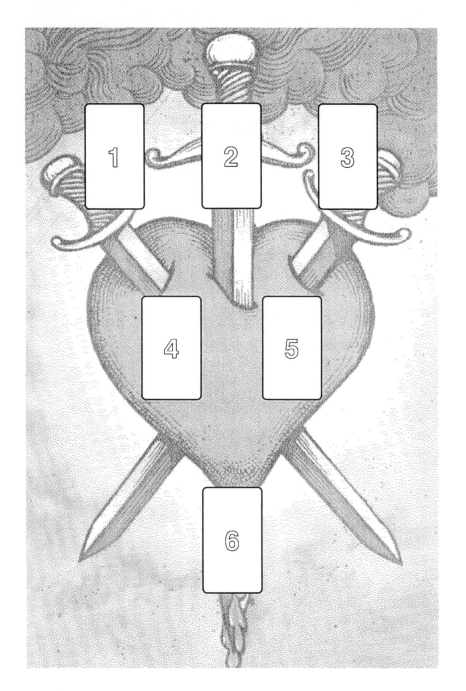

The Consequences

- I feel that I am being treated unjustly by my partner -

1. The problem

2. Why I feel that I am being treated unjustly

3. What is the deeper cause for this?

4. Is it possible that my partner is right?

5. How can I — or shall I — change my attitude?

6. How this change will influence our partnership

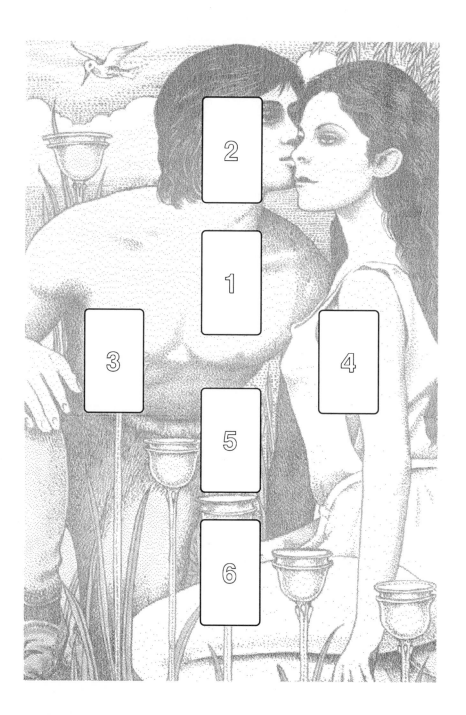

Partnership

- Separation -

1. How do I currently see the situation of the partnership?

2. What do I wish for?

3. What calls for a separation?

4. What indicates that we should stay together?

5. What shall I do?

6. What does the oracle recommend?

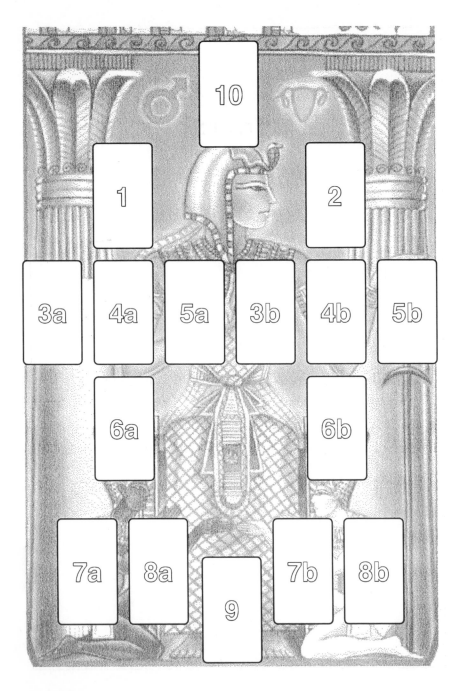

Fulfilled Partnership

This reading can be done with two people, but it can also be done alone.

1. How do I look at this partnership?

2. How does my partner look at it?

3a. Where do I make myself dependent?
   b. Where does my partner make himself or herself dependent?

4a. Where am I looking for freedom?
   b. Where is my partner looking for freedom?

5a. What kind of anxiety is gripping me?
   b. What kind of anxiety is gripping my partner?

6a. What is the path I want to follow?
   b. What is the path my partner wants to follow?

7a. Advantages of my path for myself
   b. Advantages of the path for my partner

8a. Disadvantages of my path for me
   b. Disadvantages of the path for my partner

9. What path is good for both of us?

10. What does the oracle say?

The Karmic Connection

1. The meaning of the relationship

2. My karmic inheritance

3. The karmic inheritance of my partner

4. Our former communion

5. My current task

6. The current task of my partner

7. What does my partner mean to me?

8. What do I mean to my partner?

9. What can I do for the relationship?

10. What can my partner do for the relationship?

11. Where will our relationship lead?

The Magic Wand

- aid in decision making -

1. The problem

2. This is what I want

3. This is what I need to do

4. And these are the consequences

5. This is an alternative

6. And the consequences of that alternative

7. This is what the oracle says

The Dilemma

1. This is the question I am obsessed with

2. What will happen if I do it?

3. What will happen if I don't do it, or if I do something different?

4. This feeling will result if I do it

5. This feeling will result if I don't do it

6. This is how my surroundings will help me if I do it

7. This is how my surroundings will help me if I don't do it

8. This is how it will continue if I do it

9. This is how it will continue if I don't do it

10. Advice of the Tarot

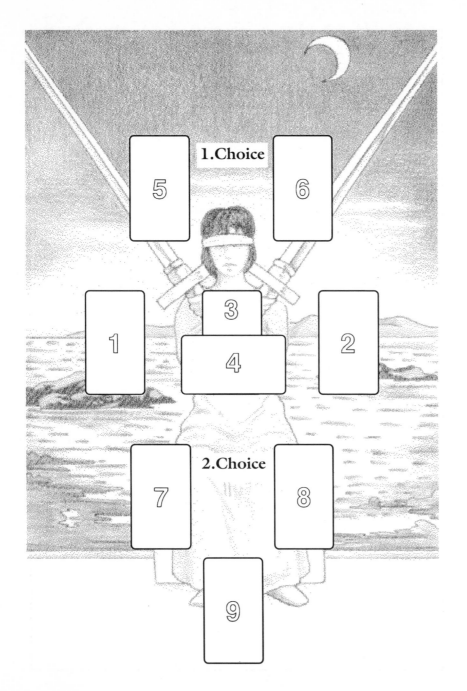

The Two Possibilities

1. My current situation

2. My prospects

3. What do my feelings tell me?

4. How shall I treat them?

5. This is the first possibility

6. What can I expect if I choose this alternative?

7. This is my second possibility

8. What can I expect if I choose this alternative?

This combination of cards can be repeated, if you have further questions.

9. Sum of the Digits Card (see page 13)

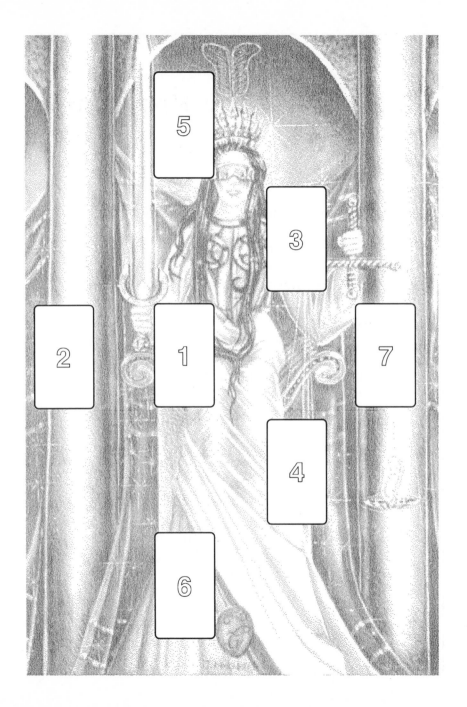

The Decision

1. This is my current situation

2. This is the reason the situation has come about

3. This can happen if I change something (it can get better or worse)

4. This can happen if I change nothing and leave things as they are (it can get better or worse)

5. These are my aids or warnings concerning actions or attitudes on my part

6. This is my task

   It can be obstacles to advancement I have to overcome

7. The Tarot's advice on which path to follow

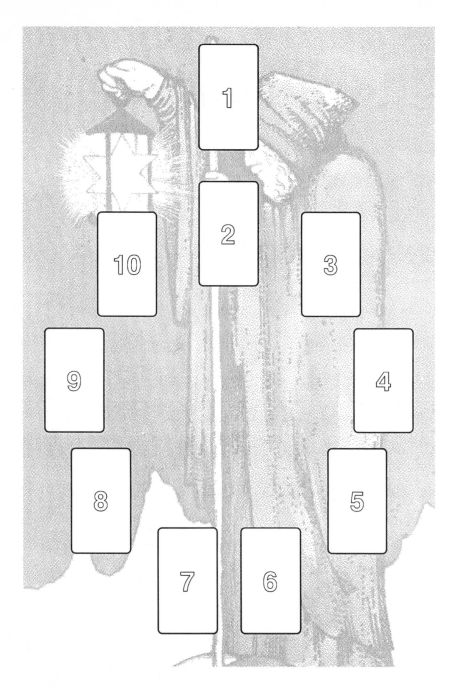

Clarifying the Problem

1. Reflecting on my question/problem

2. Where am I on top of the situation?

3. Where do I need to listen to my intuition?

4. Where is "peace at any price" not an alternative? Where do I have to assert myself?

5. Where does tolerance help me along?

6. Where am I blind to dangers?

7. Where does my excessive caution paralyze me?

8. What kind of advice should I accept?

9. Where do I have to wait patiently?

10. What do I need to do?

How Do I Come Across?

1. My situation/my problem

2. My thinking

3. My feeling

4. My actions

5. Where and how can I use my positive vibrations?

6. Where and how can I overcome my negative vibrations?

7. What will be the outcome?

The Law of Analogy

- *problem solving* -

1. My theme/my problem

2. How do I experience it?

3. How do I see the other?

4. What does he or she reflect of myself?

5. What kind of critique or weakness results from this?

6. What do I need to do?
   How can I detach myself?

7. What will I gain?

The Law of the Spirit

- *problem solving* -

1. My problem/the theme

2. The cause of my problem in the realm of the soul

3. My spiritual tasks

4. My material tasks

5. What will happen if I confront my task?

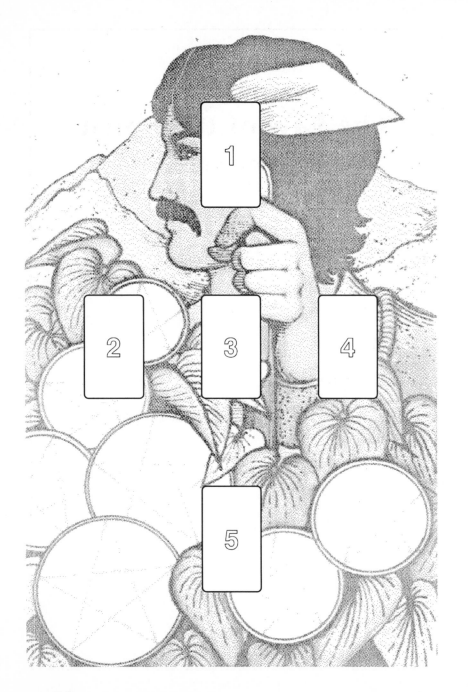

Identification (Recognition)

- cause and effect -

1. My theme/the overall situation or a special problem

2. What did I sow?

3. What did I reap?

4. What did I learn from this?

5. How shall I go on?

Identification (Recognition)

- openness -

1. This is the way I am

2. This is what I would like

3. This is what I must change
   What do I have to change?

4. These are the consequences

The Solution to the Problem

- the game of fate -

1. My problem/the theme

2. What I cannot change

3. What I need to do/my task

4. What alternative do I still have?

5. Sum of the Digits Card
   How will it continue for now?

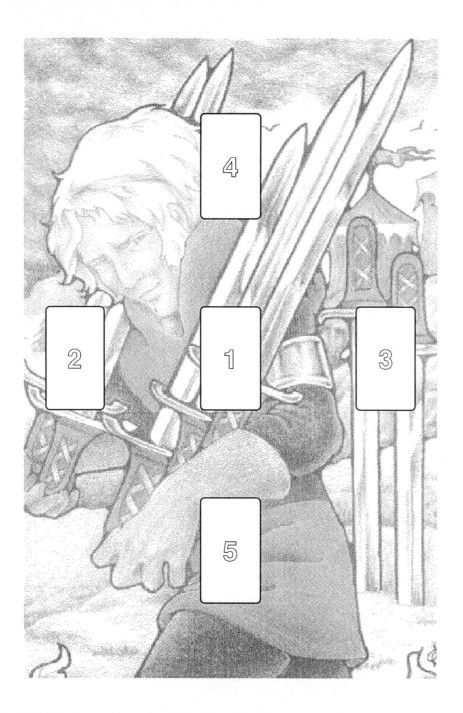

The State of Affairs

1. My current situation

2. What does my past have to do with the present?

   Why did this situation come about at all?

3. What could the future bring that could clarify the situation?

4. How do I get out of the situation?

5. How do I protect myself in this situation?

   Sum of the Digits Card:
   What will result from all of this?

Where Am I?

1. My situation/my problem
   (Consciously choose this card from the open Tarot deck.)

2. What I hope for

3. What I fear

4. What I expect the outcome to be

5. My powers, which I truly command

6. What kind of obstacles are in my path?

7. What will the outcome truly be like?

8. Advice of the Tarot

   (Use the Sum of the Digits Card, or pick a card.)

Insight

- resolving the conflict -

1. Where do I feel guilty?

2. What guilt, as I see it, is borne by the other person?

3. What kind of solution would I like?

4. What kind of solution would the other person like?

5. In what areas do I need to pull myself together?

6. Where does tolerance help?

   Where do I have a greater understanding of the weakness of the other person?

7. Where do I need to be cautious?

   Where does danger lie?

8. What is the first step I can take to resolve the conflict?

9. What will be the outcome of that step?

10. What will I gain from this?

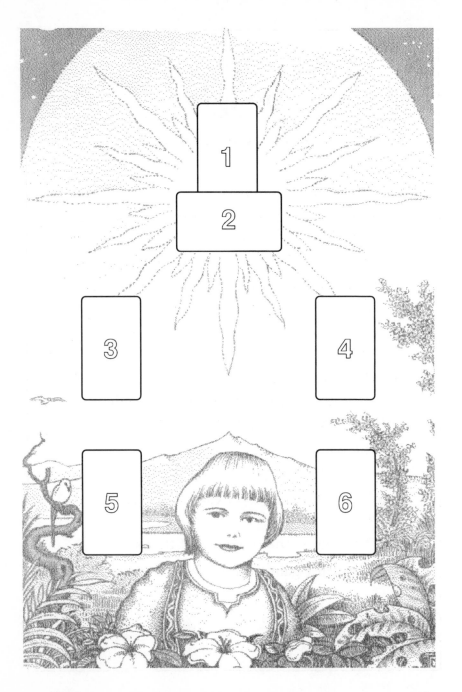

The Awakening of the Inner Child

1. My problem

2. How does my inner child look at it?

3. Which path — to the inner child — have I obstructed?

4. How can I open the path to my inner child?

5. How can I convert this to a resolution of the conflict?

6. What will I gain?

Wish Fulfillment

1. My wish
   (Look for the card that most represents your wish.)

2. What can others do for me in regard to my wish?

3. What in my surroundings prevents my wish from coming true?

4. What do I have to do to make my wish come true?

5. How am I unconsciously preventing the realization of my wish?

6. What will I gain if my wish does come true?

7. What will the realization of my wish cost me?

What will I have to sacrifice?

What do I have to expect?

General Oracle

1. My situation

2. Its negative and positive aspects

3. What can I do?
   Shall I do anything?

4. What will happen if I do nothing?

5. How will the situation change if I do something?

6. What is the advice of the oracle?

Oracle Game

1. My situation/my problem

2. This is how it arose

3. This is how I feel today

4. This will happen in the future

5. This is what the oracle warns about

6. This is what the oracle recommends

The Coin

- larger acquisitions -

1. How do I feel about the planned purchase?

2. Do I have the financial means?
   Where can I get the financial means?

3. What do I have to do?
   What obstacles do I have to overcome?

4. Will the purchase bring the contentment I wish for?

The Celtic Cross

- undertakings — like journeys and rest cures, among others -

1. How am I at the moment?

2. From whom or what do I want to escape?

3. What will I be taking along?

4. What will I be leaving behind?

5. What will await me on my return?

6. Who or what will be supportive during my stay?

7. How will I be during my stay?

8. What will the surroundings be like (the people and places)?

9. What do I hope for or fear during my stay?

10. What can I achieve by my journey?

11. What is the theme I want to think about during my stay?

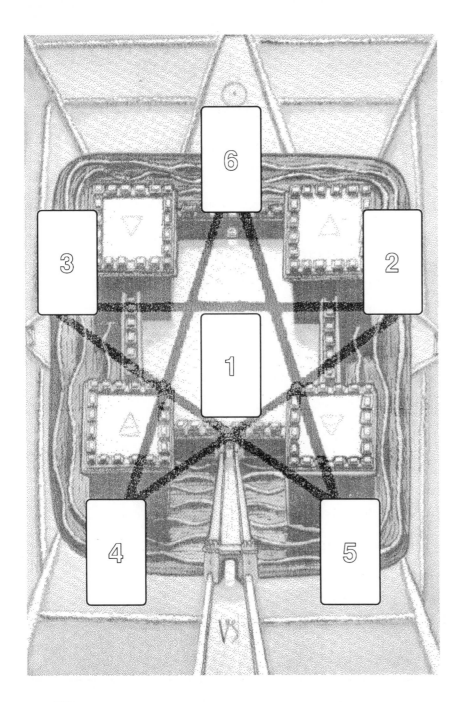

The Four Elements

1. This is my overall situation

2. The place of fire
   This is what I encounter at work

3. The place of water
   This is what I encounter in love

4. The place of the air
   This is the state of my health

5. The place of the earth
   This is my financial situation

6. This is my prophecy
   This advice is being given to me

The Star

- how can I progress in my environment? -

1. Where do I stand at the moment?

2. How can I reach my goal?

3. Obstacles I am putting in the way of others

4. Help I am getting from my higher self

5. Help others are giving me

6. Obstacles I am putting in my own path

7. My highest goal at the moment

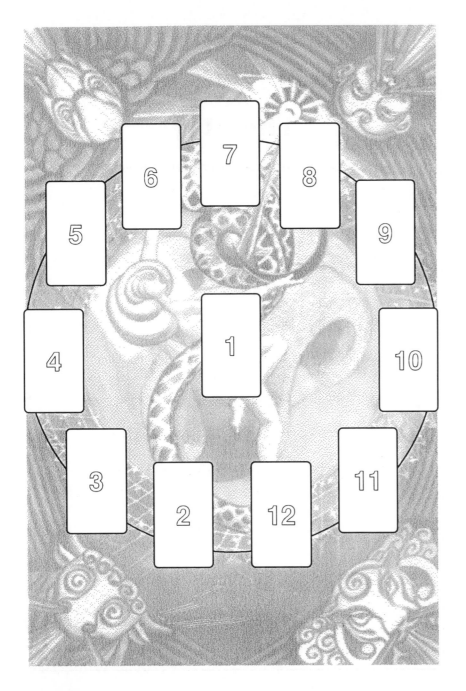

The Star of Life

1. My position in life

2. Into what time/environment/circumstances have I been born?

3. What family did I choose?

4. What kind of friends and acquaintances did I choose?

5. What are the circumstances of my life (occupation/education/environment)?

6. Whom did I choose for a life partner?

7. What crises and difficulties are in my life?

8. What high points and strengths are in my life?

9. What circumstances of life are planned for me?

10. My wishful thinking (dreams)

11. What prevents me from living the life I planned or wished for?

12. How can I achieve that life?

The Tree of Life

- *my world* -

Use only the cards of the Major Arcana for this layout.

1. My belief

2. My father

3. My mother

4. My friends

5. My enemies

6. I myself

7. My lover

8. My colleagues

9. My teacher

10. My surroundings/Where do I live?

0. My task

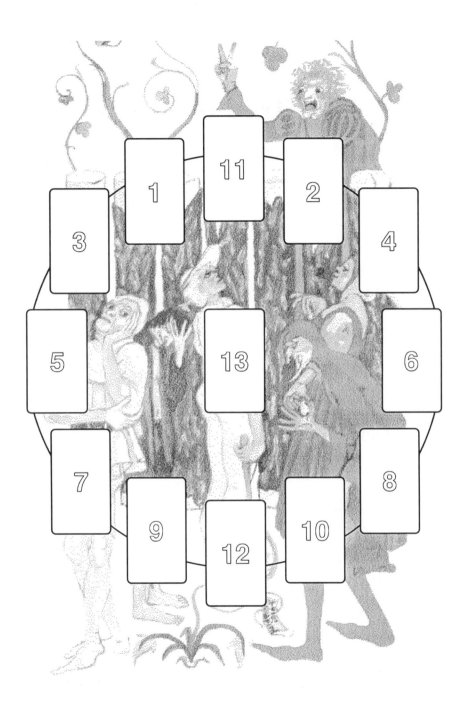

The Marketplace

1. How much of a gossip am I?

2. How much, in my opinion, do others like to gossip?

3. How much do I look to others for leadership?

4. How much, in my opinion, do others look to me for leadership?

5. How strongly do I criticize others?

6. How strongly do I think others criticize me?

7. How much do I take advantage of others?

8. How much do others take advantage of me?

9. How strong is my true interest in others?

10. How strong, as I see it, are others interested in me?

11. How can I free myself from this interplay?

12. Would I like to free myself from this interplay?

13. How can I better reach my center? How self-righteous am I?

Occupational Oracle

1. My occupation

2. This opposes me in my occupation

3. My conscious wish

4. What is the actuality here?

5. How do I feel unconsciously?

6. What will happen to me in the future from an occupational point of view?

7. What will I gain?

8. Can I realize my dreams?

   How will it continue?

The Higher Position

- shall I run for office? -
- shall I ask for a promotion? -

Use this reading whenever you are trying to advance from your current position to a higher position.

1. My wish

2. My doubts

3. What can I do for my subordinates?

4. How are my abilities or my prerequisites for this job?

5. What do I still have to learn?

6. What kind of commitment will I have to make?

7. What "bitter pill" will I have to swallow if I get this position?

8. What are my successes?

9. What do I truly want to achieve from this position?
(Be honest!)

10. Can I realize the highest ideals I want to achieve with the help of this position?

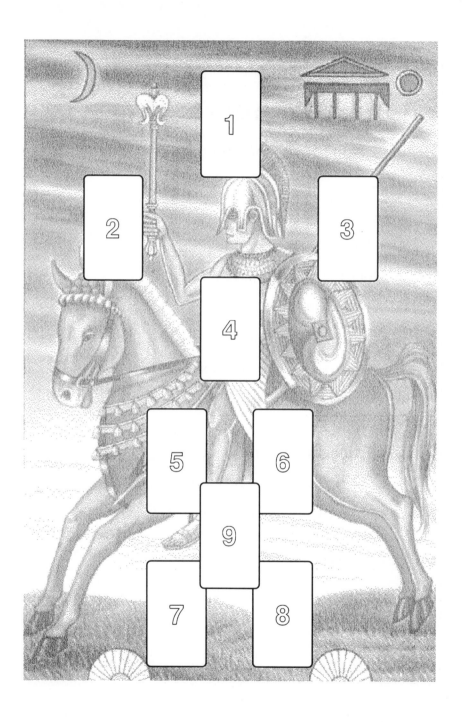

Occupational Decision

- shall I change jobs? -

1. My current job situation

2. This is what I like about it
   This is what makes me discontent

3. This is why my employer is happy with me/not happy with me

4. This is my innermost wish

5.+ 6. What is favorable to a change?

7.+ 8. What speaks for staying?

9. This is what the oracle advises

The Undertaking

- the collaboration -

1. What is the project like?

2. Does the project make sense?

3. What is my mistake?

4. What kind of mistake is the other making?

5. What positive contribution can I make?

6. What positive contribution can the other make?

7. The outcome of the project

8. This card will be drawn after all the others:

   Are the two partners capable of doing something that will prevent a negative outcome for the project?

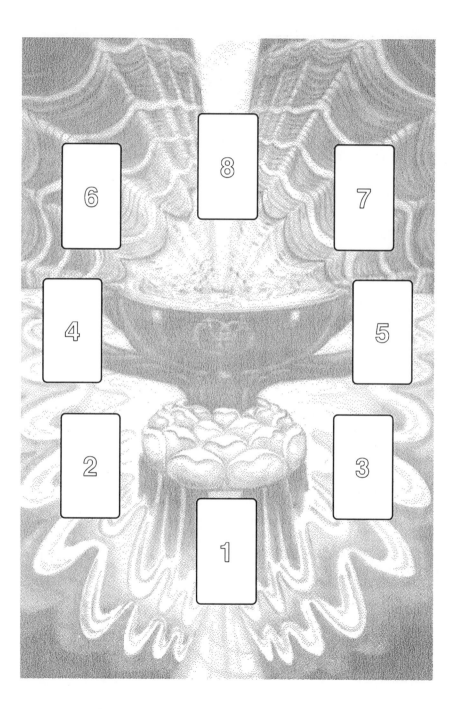

The Cup of Luck and Success

1. Where in my life would I like to have more success?

   "The problem"

2. Where do I need to apply myself more?

3. Where do I use too much of the wrong kind of energy?

4. Where do I doubt myself or my capabilities?

5. Where am I arrogant?

   Where do I think I'm better than I am?

6. Where is my thinking too negative?

   Am I charging myself with destructive energy — and experiencing it coming back to me?

7. Whom or what should I forgive?

   How do I recharge myself?

   In what area do I need to think positively?

8. How can I seize the opportunity/my luck?

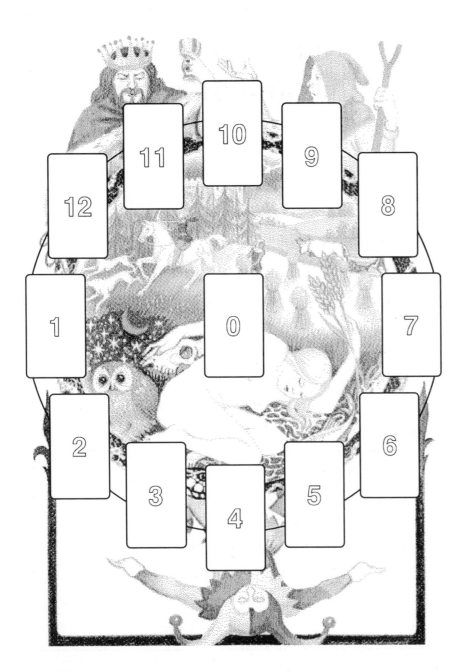

The Astrological Signs

Do this reading in two parts. Divide the Tarot cards into two stacks, Major Arcana and Minor Arcana. Before you begin the reading, select a card that will represent you.

0 My significant card

Check the table of birth dates (pages 15) and select the card that is listed for your birthday. Take out the corresponding Court Card.

Shuffle the first 12 cards from the Major Arcana and put them in place. These cards represent your inner state of development. Then fill the circle once more with the shuffled cards from the Minor Arcana. Numbered cards will show you how you are currently living in this state of development. Court Cards will show you through whom you are living.

1. What do I bring to this life (my mental attitudes, my options, my character, my role)?

2. How do I experience luxury (my financial situation, my possessions, my waste)?

3. My curiosity (small changes in residence, interests, my versatility)

4. What makes me feel secure (my home, family)?

5. How willing am I to take risks (games, fun, romantic involvements, speculations)?

6. How well do I examine things (attention to detail, work, health)?

7. My security (contracts, partnership, marriage)

8. How will I leave life?
   Am I open to spiritual matters (the beyond, the occult)?

9. How wide-ranging are my interests (higher education, religion, further journeys)?

10. My occupation (How does it give me satisfaction?)
    Do I live according to my calling?

11. How do I use my free time?
    What kinds of friends do I gather around me?

12. How do I experience confinement (isolation, imprisonment, addiction)?

Aries

♈

-I am -

1. How am I?
   My appearance

2. How is my vitality?

3. How is my ability to succeed?
   How is my uncontrollable side?

4. How is my enthusiasm?

5. What am I escaping from?

6. How do I need to approach my goals?

7. What do I want?

Taurus

♉

- I have -

1. My attitude towards possessions and money

2. The current state of my finances

3. Abilities and talents that are currently at my disposal

4. The state of my sensual pleasure

5. The state of my desire for excess and luxuries

6. How much patience I have
   My being rooted

7. How possessive and jealous am I?

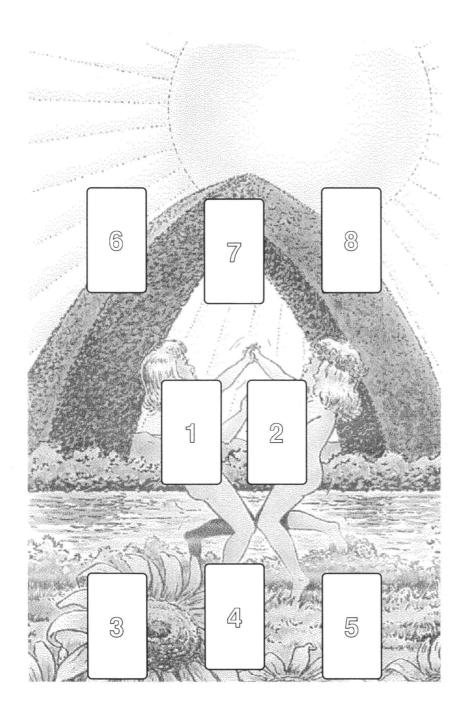

Gemini

♊

- I think -

1. How is my mind working currently?

2. How is my ability to lie?

3. How and what am I studying?

4. How do I get along with my neighbors and siblings?

5. How do I communicate with others? Do I get involved in dissension and intrigues?

6. What do I doubt?

7. What flights of fancy do I experience?

8. What does my inner twin look like?

Cancer

♋

- I feel -

1. Where do I come from?

2. What are my dreams?

3. How is my current home?

4. This is how I see my father

5. This is my need for security

6. How do I express my feelings?

7. How caring am I?

8. How is my mediumistic ability?

Leo

♌

- I want -

1. My ego
   How domineering am I?

2. On what stage am I acting?

3. My inner child

4. Where do I stand in regard to love and romance?

5. My love for children

6. Do I love risk and speculation?

7. My crown
   How generous am I?

Virgo
♍

- I analyze -

1. My attitude towards my body

2. My interest in medicine

3. How is my current physical health?

4. My attitude towards work

5. How is my ability for critical examination?

6. How do I adjust?

7. How hypocritical and "perfect" am I?

8. How cautious and distanced am I?

Libra

♎

- I balance -

1. My power of decision making

2. My ability to bond in a relationship

3. My ability to connect in a professional collaboration

4. My aggression and my desire for peace
   How do I fight?

5. My will to forgive
   How do I make peace?
   How vindictive am I?

6. What do I give to my lover?

7. What kind of feelings do I suppress?

8. How is my artistic feeling?

9. How superficial am I?
   How moody am I?

Scorpio

♏

- I desire -

1. My tendency to suppress

2. My taboos

3. My sexuality

4. How do I see my death?

5. My values

6. Inheritances awaiting me

7. My tendency towards self-destruction

8. My profundity/depth

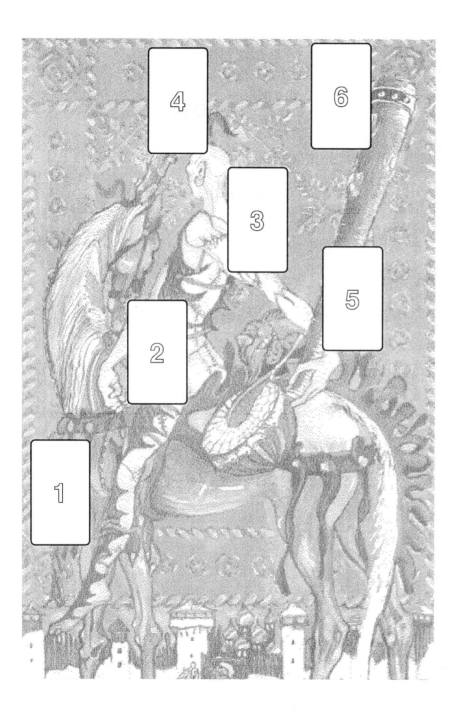

Sagittarius

♐

- I see -

1. This is my current social environment

2. This is my education up to now

3. This is my religion, my belief, and also my self-righteousness

4. My journeys in the outer world

5. My journeys in the inner world

6. My search for meaning

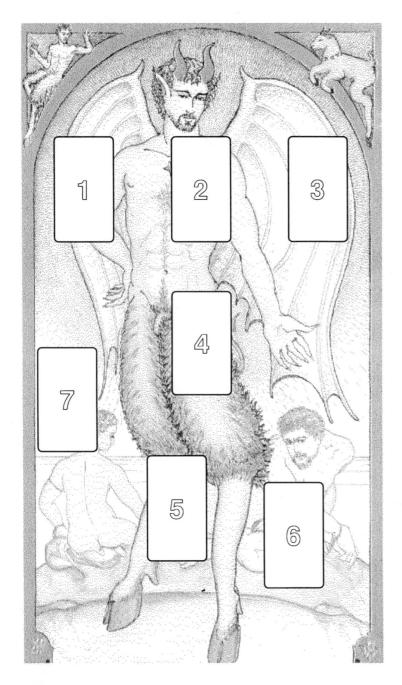

Capricorn

♑

- I use -

1. My career

2. My desire for power and fame

3. How responsible and serious am I?

4. My relationship to the current value system

5. This is how I see my mother

6. What position in society can I reach?

7. What am I developing towards?

Aquarius

- I know -

1. These are my current friends

2. How is my desire for freedom?

3. Do I claim leadership in the group?

4. How do I oppose society?

5. How is my spontaneity?

6. This is my feeling of inferiority

7. Do I overestimate myself?

8. How do I reach the star?
   Can I live my dreams?

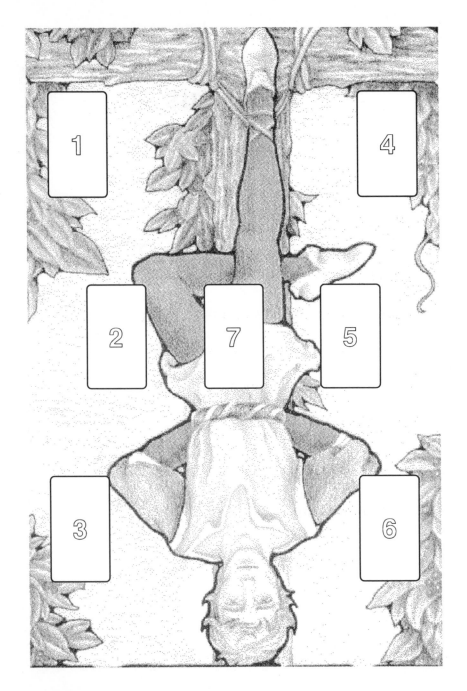

Pisces

♓

- I believe -

1. My idealism

2. My willingness to sacrifice

3. My spiritual experience

4. My addiction to . . .

5. My current secret enemies

6. My prison
   Where am I bound/stuck?

7. What will deliver me of my burdens?

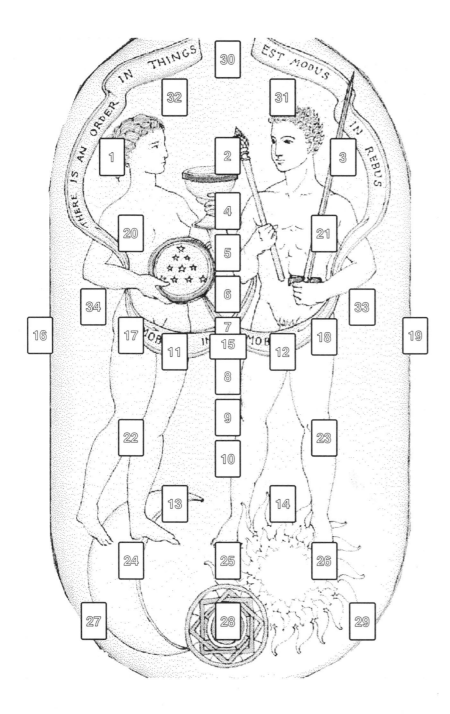

The Structure of Life

- the total human being -

GENERAL CONDITION

1. Body
2. Mind
3. Soul

CHAKRAS/HEALTH

4. Opening for the spiritual/brain
5. Perception/senses
6. Ability to make contact/lungs
7. Ability to love/heart
8. Boundaries/digestion
9. Creativity/sexuality
10. Letting go/organs of elimination

MINOR CHAKRAS

11. Acting/intervention
12. Letting things happen
13. Moving on
14. Point of view/prejudice

RELATIONSHIPS

15. Lover
16. Connections from the past
17. Connections from the past that reach into the present
18. Connections that reach into the future
19. Connections that will arise in the future

THE FOUR ELEMENTS/ THE FOUR SUITS OF THE TAROT

20. Occupation/enterprise
21. Love/friendship
22. Conflicts/disputes
23. Security/money

GOALS IN LIFE

24. Task
25. Ability
26. Possibility

THE INNER CHILD

27. Injuries in childhood
28. What is their effect today?
29. How can they be healed?

BRANCHES ON THE TREE OF LIFE

30. Goal/divine guidance
31. Spiritual guidance/wisdom
32. Intelligence
33. Grace/charity/mildness
34. Power/severity

Acknowledgments

The illustrations on the following pages are reprinted with the kind permission of the manufacturer, U.S. Games Systems, Inc., Stamford, CT 06902, USA. Further reproduction is not permitted:

Aquarian Tarot, © 1970 by U.S. Games Systems, Inc.: 75

Art Nouveau Tarot, © 1988 by U.S. Games Systems, Inc.: 76

Chinese Tarot Deck, © 1989 by U.S. Games Systems, Inc.: 40, 68

Connolly Tarot Deck, © 1970 by U.S. Games Systems, Inc.: 26, 63, 88

Hanson-Roberts Tarot Deck, © 1985 by U.S. Games Systems, Inc.: 29, 35, 37, 61, 92

Medieval Scapini Tarot, © 1985 by U.S. Games Systems, Inc.: 20, 74, 89

Morgan Greer Tarot, © 1979 by U.S. Games Systems, Inc.: 18, 30, 44, 46, 54, 56, 58, 60, 69

Renaissance Tarot Deck, © 1987 by U.S. Games Systems, Inc.: 90, 91, 93

Tarot of the Ages, © 1988 by U.S. Games Systems, Inc.: 28

Universal Waite Tarot Deck, © 1991 by U.S. Games Systems, Inc.: 36, 43, 52, 57, 65, 73

The illustrations on the following pages are reprinted with the kind permission of Ansata Verlag, Interlaken, Switzerland:

Mertz-Struck Tarot, Ansata Verlag: 16, 51

The illustrations on the following pages are reprinted by the kind permission of AGM AGMueller, CH-8212 Neuhausen am Rheinfall, Switzerland:

Arcus Arcanum Tarot, AGM AGMueller, Neuhausen: 19, 39, 66, 81, 82, 83, 84, 85, 87

Chinesisches Tarot, AGM AGMueller, Neuhausen: 41, 49

Crowley Original Thoth Tarot Karten, AGM AGMuller, Neuhausen: 17, 28, 33, 34, 70, 72, 78, 79, 86

Ibis Tarot, AGM AGMuller, Neuhausen: 22, 23, 48, 77

Weise Frauen Tarot, AGM AGMuller, Neuhausen: 31, 42, 50, 55, 59, 62, 71, 80

The illustrations on the following pages are reprinted from the Cosmic Tarot with the kind permission of the Walter Holl Agency, 52078, Aachen, Germany:

Cosmic Tarot, F.X. Schmid: 21, 32, 45, 47, 64, 67

The illustration on the following page is reprinted from the Voyager Tarot with the kind permission of Integral, Verlages, Volkar-Magnum, Verlagsgesellschaft mbH, Germany:

Voyager Tarot, Integral, Verlages: 27

The illustrations on the following pages are reprinted from the Eclectic Tarot with the kind permission of Wiener Spielkartenfabrik Ferd. Piatnik & Soehne, Germany:

Eclectic Tarot, Wiener Spielkartenfabrik Ferd. Piatnik & Soehne: 24, 25, 53

About the Authors

Markus Schirner gives courses in the pendulum and in the Tarot. He is head of the Center for Kinesiology in Darmstadt, Germany, where he also teaches.

Astrologer Heidemarie Pielmeier has been giving courses in the Tarot for beginning and advanced students for over 14 years. She also prepares personalized Tarot profiles and Bach Flower Analyses.

INDEX